Analogies

Grades 4-5

by Linda Ward Beech

SCHOLASTIC
PROFESSIONAL **B**OOKS

New York · Toronto · London · Auckland · Sydney
Mexico City · New Delhi · Hong Kong · Buenos Aires

Cover design by Andrew Jenkins and Kelli Thompson
Cover illustration by Kate Flanagan
Interior design by Glenn Davis
Interior illustrations by Maxie Chambliss and Kate Flanagan

ISBN 0-439-27173-8

Contents

To the Teacher

Why Teach Analogies?

Analogies explore word—and therefore concept—relationships. Implicit in making analogies are numerous critical-thinking skills. It is for these reasons that analogies appear on so many standardized tests.

Teaching analogies offers important and concrete benefits to students. Working with analogies:

✦ expands students' vocabulary.

✦ directs students to recognize different shades of word meanings.

✦ helps students understand relationships between words and ideas.

✦ reinforces students' ability to make comparisons.

✦ causes students to read more carefully.

✦ develops reasoning skills.

✦ prepares students for standardized tests.

Using the Book

The reproducible pages in this book provide step-by-step instruction in introducing and practicing different kinds of analogies. Students review the thinking skill needed for understanding each kind of analogy and become familiar with the formats in which the analogies appear. The THINK! component at the bottom of each page directs students to explain and explore their reasoning.

As you introduce each type of analogy or format, you'll want to model how to do it by thinking aloud. See the sample Think Alouds for each section. Be sure to provide dictionaries and/or thesauruses for students to use as they work on the analogies.

Teacher Tip

Working in pairs or small groups gives students the opportunity to try out and explain their thinking as they work on analogies.

Examining Similarities (pages 8–11)

Analogies require that students recognize similarities in order to categorize words and ideas. Pages 8–9 provide practice in different kinds of grouping activities. Pages 10–11 require students to focus on the similarities between pairs of things.

Same Class Relationships (pages 12–16)

Page 12 Before students begin to recognize same class relationships, they need to understand that class means the same as group. This page gives students practice in recognizing things in the same group.

Teacher Tip

Remind students as often as necessary to read all the choices for an analogy before writing an answer.

Page 13 Read the tip and remind students that if the first pair of words in an analogy names things in the same class, the second pair of words must also follow this pattern. Point out that the first and second word pairs don't usually name things in the same class, however. For example, if the first pair names two kinds of animals, the second pair might name two kinds of mushrooms. If students ask about the symbol [::], explain that it is sometimes used to separate the two sets or pairs in an analogy.

Think Aloud

A rat and a shrew are both kinds of rodents, so they are in the same class. A cobra is a snake which is a reptile so I need to find another snake or reptile. The first choice is cat. No, a cat isn't a reptile. A mouse? A snake might eat a mouse but a mouse is not in the same class as a reptile. A boa constrictor? Yes, a boa constrictor is another kind of snake, so it's in the same class as a cobra.

Page 14 Read the tip. Tell students that analogies are sometimes stated with the words *is to*. Point out that although some of the answer choices relate to the first word pair, they are incorrect. Stress that the answer must be a word that relates to the third underlined word in the same way as the first two words relate.

Page 15 Read the tip. Explain that the first pair of words is linked by this symbol [:]. The symbol [::] appears between the first and second pair of words. For each item, have students repeat a sentence similar to the one given in the tip.

Page 16 On this page students must choose a word pair to complete the analogy. Remind students to look for a word pair in which the words are related in the same way as the first word pair.

Part/Whole Relationships (pages 17–22)

Page 17 Before students begin to recognize part/whole relationships, they need to understand what these are. This page provides an introduction to the concept by asking students to explain how the words in each analogy are related.

Page 18 This page reinforces the use of the part/whole sentence.

Page 19 This page provides practice using analogies with the "is to" format.

Think Aloud

A statue is something you might see in a museum, so it is part of a museum. A dictionary is part of a what? A library? That seems like a good choice, but I'll read the other choices before I decide. A student? No, a student uses a dictionary but a dictionary isn't part of a student. A book? No, a dictionary is a book but isn't part of one. I'll go back to the first choice—library. That makes the most sense.

Page 20 Read the tip. Review the symbol [:] and explain that it stands for the words *is to*. Review the symbol [::] and explain that it stands for the word *as*.

Page 21 On this page students must choose a word pair to complete the analogy. Remind students to look for a word pair in which the words are related in the same way as the first word pair.

Page 22 This page reviews same class and part/whole analogies. Remind students of the importance of understanding the relationship of the first two words in the analogy.

Synonyms (pages 23–28)

Page 23 Before students begin to recognize synonym relationships, they need to understand what these are. This page provides practice using synonyms.

Page 24 This page reinforces the concept of synonyms.

Page 25 This page provides practice using analogies with the "is to" format.

Think Aloud

A path is another word for trail so this is a synonym analogy. I need to find another word for fun. Amusement? That seems like a possible choice but I'll read the other choices to be sure. Work? No, work is the opposite of fun. Hike? No, hike is something you do on a path or trail, but it is not a synonym for fun. I think amusement is the best choice.

Page 26 Read the tip. Review the symbol [:] and explain that it stands for the words *is to*. Review the symbol [::] and explain that it stands for the word *as*.

Page 27 On this page students must choose a word pair to complete the analogy. Remind students to look for a word pair in which the words are related in the same way as the first word pair.

Page 28 This page reviews same class, part/whole, and synonym analogies. Remind students of the importance of understanding the relationship of the first two words in the analogy.

Antonyms (pages 29–34)

Page 29 Before students begin to recognize antonym relationships, they need to understand what these are. This page provides practice using antonyms.

Page 30 This page reinforces the concept of antonyms.

Teacher Tip

Suggest that students predict what the answer might be before they look at the answer choices, then look to see if their guess is there. Remind students that if the exact word isn't given as a choice, they should look for a synonym.

Page 31 This page provides practice using analogies with the "is to" format.

Think Aloud

Valuable means the opposite of worthless so this is an antonym analogy. I need to find the opposite of comic. Funny? No, funny is similar to comic; it's not the opposite. Tragic? Yes, tragic is the opposite of comic, but I'll read the last choice to be sure. Worthy? No, worthy is the opposite of worthless, but not the opposite of comic. That's a tricky choice! The answer is tragic.

Page 32 Read the tip. Review the symbol [:] and explain that it stands for the words *is to*. Review the symbol [::] and explain that it stands for the word *as*.

Page 33 On this page students must choose a word pair to complete the analogy. Remind students to look for a word pair in which the words are related in the same way as the first word pair.

Page 34 This page reviews same class, part/whole, synonym, and antonym analogies. Remind students of the importance of understanding the relationship of the first two words in the analogy.

Homophones (pages 35–40)

Page 35 Before students begin to recognize homophone relationships, they need to understand what these are. This page provides an introduction to the concept.

Teacher Tip

Because of different accents and dialects, students may need pronunciation help with homophones.

Page 36 This page reinforces the concept of homophones.

Page 37 This page provides practice using analogies with the "is to" format.

Think Aloud

New and *knew* are homophones because they sound alike and have different spellings and different meanings. So the relationship in this analogy is homophones and I need to find a homophone for the word *side*. The word *know* is related to knew, but it is not a homophone for side. Whole? A side might be part of a whole, but that is not the relationship I need. Sighed? Yes, sighed is a homophone for side; it sounds the same, but is spelled differently and has a different meaning.

Think Aloud

Five is an example of a number so bus must be an example of what? Riders? No, riders use a bus but that's not the relationship I need. Vehicle? That's the word I was thinking of; a bus is an example of a vehicle. But I'm going to read the last choice just in case. Cars? No, a car is also an example of a vehicle, but car isn't the name of the class. Vehicle is the best answer.

Page 38 Read the tip. Review the symbol [:] and explain that it stands for the words *is to*. Review the symbol [::] and explain that it stands for the word *as*.

Page 39 On this page students must choose a word pair to complete the analogy. Remind students to look for a word pair in which the words are related in the same way as the first word pair.

Page 40 This page reviews same class, part/whole, synonym, antonym, and homophone analogies. Remind students of the importance of understanding the relationship of the first two words in the analogy.

Class and Example (pages 41–47)

Page 41 Before students begin to recognize class and example relationships, they need to understand what these are. This page provides an introduction to the concept.

Page 42 This page reinforces the concept of class and example relationships.

Page 43 This page provides practice using analogies with the "is to" format.

Page 44 Read the tip. Review the symbol [:] and explain that it stands for the words *is to*. Review the symbol [::] and explain that it stands for the word *as*.

Page 45 On this page students must choose a word pair to complete the analogy. Remind students to look for a word pair in which the words are related in the same way as the first word pair.

Pages 46–47 These pages serve as a final review of same class, part/whole, synonym, antonym, homophone, and class and example analogies. Remind students of the importance of understanding the relationship of the first two words in the analogy.

Examining Similarities

Group Names

Decide how the words in each group are alike. On the blank line write a word that names the group.

1. _____
   poodle
   collie
   beagle

2. _____
   rainy
   snowy
   sunny

3. _____
   cider
   milk
   juice

4. _____
   nose
   lips
   eyes

5. _____
   beef
   ham
   veal

6. _____
   pint
   gallon
   quart

7. _____
   mountain
   valley
   plain

8. _____
   rectangle
   rhombus
   triangle

THINK!
Think of another example to go in each group.

Examining Similarities

Group and Regroup

Find the word in each box that doesn't belong. Cross it out,
then write it on the last line in the box where it does belong.

1.
fall
inform
swoop
drop
descend
tumble

_____

2.
osprey
heron
stamen
emu
petrel
kingfisher

_____

3.
teach
tell
notify
impart
instruct
pond

_____

4.
pollen
stigma
ovule
temple
pistil
petal

_____

5.
shrine
pagoda
mosque
cathedral
church
macaw

_____

6.
bay
lagoon
topple
inlet
lake
gulf

_____

THINK!
Tell a partner how the words
in each box go together.

Examining Similarities

A Close Look

Explain how the things in each pair are alike.

1. kite and balloon _____

_____

2. watch and clock _____

_____

3. magazine and newspaper _____

_____

4. piano and accordion _____

_____

5. pond and lake _____

_____

6. highway and street _____

_____

7. bunk and hammock _____

_____

8. bonnet and cap _____

_____

 THINK!
Compare your answers with a partner's. • • • • • • •

Examing Similarities

Picking Pairs

For each number, a line connects two things that go together. Find two other things that go together in the same way. Draw a line to connect them.

1. imaginary   number
   ban   make-believe
   allow   forbid

2. secret   midnight
   huge ——————————— tiny
   solid   liquid

3. clap   permit
   prevent   applaud
   allow   pretend

4. terrier   retriever
   lime ——————————— strawberry
   penguin   crowd

5. core   see
   time   hear
   here   corps

6. snake   mammal
   tiger   jungle
   skin   reptile

7. perfect ———————— flawless
   puppy   stare
   stroll   walk

8. chair   candle
   wick   soft
   cord   lamp

THINK!
Tell a partner how the pairs you matched go together.

11

Same Class

Into Groups

Read each group of words in List 1. Decide how the words are alike. Then find a name for the group in List 2. Write the letter of the group name on the line.

List 1	List 2
1. _____ store, school, hotel	A. flowers
2. _____ purple, yellow, orange	B. footwear
3. _____ desk, sofa, table	C. birds
4. _____ snake, lizard, alligator	D. coins
5. _____ tulip, violet, daisy	E. buildings
6. _____ slippers, boots, sandals	F. furniture
7. _____ flute, drum, violin	G. trees
8. _____ quarter, nickel, penny	H. reptiles
9. _____ birch, pine, walnut	I. colors
10. _____ goose, robin, parrot	J. musical instruments

THINK!
Think of another example to go in each group.

Same Class

Somehow Alike

Decide how the first two words go together. Choose the word that goes with the third word in the same way.

> **Tip** ✓
>
> lily and dahlia :: fork and spoon
>
>
>
> Say to yourself: The first two words are flowers so they are in the same group or class. The second word pair must name things in the same class too. The second pair of words names two utensils.

1. rat and shrew :: cobra and _____
   - Ⓐ cat
   - Ⓑ mouse
   - Ⓒ boa constrictor

2. autumn and winter :: blue and _____
   - Ⓐ brown
   - Ⓑ cold
   - Ⓒ three

3. cottage and bungalow :: gingham and _____
   - Ⓐ plaid
   - Ⓑ hut
   - Ⓒ dog

4. banjo and guitar :: canoe and _____
   - Ⓐ paddle
   - Ⓑ river
   - Ⓒ kayak

5. badminton and volleyball :: wrench and _____
   - Ⓐ soccer
   - Ⓑ hammer
   - Ⓒ factory

6. perch and halibut :: record and _____
   - Ⓐ gift
   - Ⓑ trout
   - Ⓒ CD

7. broccoli and turnip :: beret and _____
   - Ⓐ spinach
   - Ⓑ tam
   - Ⓒ golf

8. necklace and ring :: parsley and _____
   - Ⓐ dill
   - Ⓑ eat
   - Ⓒ fruit

THINK!
Explain your answers to a partner.

Same Class

Is To

The first two underlined words in each sentence name things that are in the same group or class. Read the third underlined word. Complete each sentence with a word in the same class as the third underlined word.

> **Tip** ✔
>
> A <u>queen</u> is to a <u>czar</u> as <u>baseball</u> is to <u>football</u>.
> Say to yourself: A queen and a czar are both rulers;
> baseball and football are both sports.

1. <u>Cousin</u> is to <u>aunt</u> as <u>oval</u> is to _____.
   Ⓐ egg   Ⓑ uncle   Ⓒ circle

2. A <u>biography</u> is to a <u>novel</u> as <u>coffee</u> is to _____.
   Ⓐ dark   Ⓑ tea   Ⓒ mystery

3. A <u>peach</u> is to an <u>apricot</u> as a <u>jeep</u> is to a _____.
   Ⓐ sedan   Ⓑ tire   Ⓒ plum

4. A <u>quail</u> is to a <u>pigeon</u> as a <u>butterfly</u> is to a _____.
   Ⓐ gnat   Ⓑ dove   Ⓒ flower

5. A <u>diamond</u> is to an <u>emerald</u> as a <u>hurricane</u> is to a _____.
   Ⓐ sunshine   Ⓑ ruby   Ⓒ tornado

6. A <u>pencil</u> is to a <u>pen</u> as a <u>tailor</u> is to a _____.
   Ⓐ crayon   Ⓑ shoemaker   Ⓒ thread

7. A <u>redwood</u> is to a <u>maple</u> as a <u>pumpkin</u> is to a _____.
   Ⓐ pineapple Ⓑ beet   Ⓒ birch

8. A <u>mop</u> is to a <u>broom</u> as a <u>museum</u> is to a _____.
   Ⓐ library   Ⓑ painting   Ⓒ bucket

THINK!
Tell a partner what the groups for each word pair are.

Same Class

Pick a Word

Read the first word pair. Write a word from the box to complete the second word pair.

Tip ✔

cat : dog :: doll : ball

Say to yourself: A cat and dog are both pets; a doll and a ball are both toys.

W O R D	peninsula	apple	lobster	period	**B O X**
	hoe	goat	train	mumps	

1. placemat : tablecloth :: cherry : _____

2. squirrel : chipmunk :: rake : _____

3. kitchen : bedroom :: cow : _____

4. seven : nine :: bus : _____

5. desert : jungle :: island : _____

6. coal : oil :: measles : _____

7. writer : banker :: crab : _____

8. noun : verb :: comma : _____

THINK!
Tell a partner what the groups for each word pair are.

Same Class

Pairing Up

Read each word pair. Choose the word pair that goes together in the same way.

> **Tip** ✔
>
> dress : suit :: cup : glass
> Say to yourself: A dress and suit are in the same class
> because they are both clothing. A cup and glass are in
> the same class because they are both things for drinking.

1. skateboard : ski :: _____
   Ⓐ hot : cold   Ⓑ animal : zoo   Ⓒ cotton : velvet

2. microscope : telescope :: _____
   Ⓐ sleeve : shirt   Ⓑ cook : chef   Ⓒ golf : hockey

3. trout : bass :: _____
   Ⓐ judge : court   Ⓑ red : blue   Ⓒ owl : wise

4. carnation : larkspur :: _____
   Ⓐ bulldog : chow   Ⓑ shoe : leather   Ⓒ artist : easel

5. robin : chickadee :: _____
   Ⓐ trunk : tree   Ⓑ sofa : couch   Ⓒ elm : oak

6. soldier : sailor :: _____
   Ⓐ toe : foot   Ⓑ orange : lemon   Ⓒ diary : journal

7. poem : legend :: _____
   Ⓐ milk : cow   Ⓑ sky : blue   Ⓒ puppy : kitten

8. mother : brother :: _____
   Ⓐ celery : stalk   Ⓑ student : pupil   Ⓒ corn : carrot

THINK!
Tell a partner how the word pairs you
did not choose are related.

Part/Whole Relationships

○ ○

Part of a Whole

Some things are parts of other things. For example, a page is a part of a book.
First read each sentence. Note the underlined words. Then tell how the words in the
first pair are related and how the words in the second pair are related.

> **Tip** ✔
>
> A <u>page</u> is to a <u>notebook</u> as an <u>eraser</u> is to a <u>pencil</u>.
> Say to yourself: A page is part of a notebook, and an eraser is part of a pencil.

1. A <u>map</u> is to an <u>atlas</u> as a <u>definition</u> is to a <u>dictionary</u>. _____

_____

2. A <u>wing</u> is to a <u>bird</u> as a <u>fin</u> is to a <u>fish</u>. _____

_____

3. <u>Sand</u> is to a <u>beach</u> as <u>trees</u> are to a <u>forest</u>. _____

_____

4. A <u>mattress</u> is to a <u>bed</u> as a <u>cushion</u> is to a <u>chair</u>. _____

_____

5. A <u>recipe</u> is to a <u>cookbook</u> as a <u>photo</u> is to an <u>album</u>. _____

_____

THINK!
Make up a part/whole analogy for a
partner to complete.

○ ○ ○ ○ ○ ○ ○ ○

Part/Whole Relationships

Add the Part

Choose the correct word to complete each sentence.

1. <u>Icing</u> is part of a <u>cake</u>, and <u>cheese</u> is part of a _____.
   - Ⓐ cow
   - Ⓑ pizza
   - Ⓒ candy

2. A <u>monitor</u> is part of a <u>computer</u>, and a <u>speaker</u> is part of a _____.
   - Ⓐ stereo
   - Ⓑ listener
   - Ⓒ mouse

3. An <u>entry</u> is part of a <u>diary</u>, and an <u>editorial</u> is part of a _____.
   - Ⓐ thesaurus
   - Ⓑ poem
   - Ⓒ newspaper

4. A <u>battery</u> is part of a <u>flashlight</u>, and a <u>lens</u> is part of a _____.
   - Ⓐ camera
   - Ⓑ radio
   - Ⓒ cell phone

5. A <u>city</u> is part of a <u>state</u>, and a <u>country</u> is part of a _____.
   - Ⓐ farm
   - Ⓑ town
   - Ⓒ continent

6. A <u>trombone</u> is part of a <u>band</u>, and a <u>gear</u> is part of a _____.
   - Ⓐ machine
   - Ⓑ tent
   - Ⓒ drum

7. <u>Sap</u> is part of a <u>tree</u>, and <u>juice</u> is part of a _____.
   - Ⓐ branch
   - Ⓑ lemon
   - Ⓒ milk

8. <u>Roses</u> are part of a <u>garden</u>, and <u>peas</u> are part of a _____.
   - Ⓐ green
   - Ⓑ pod
   - Ⓒ bean

THINK!
Read your answers to a partner.
Explain why you chose them.

Part/Whole Relationships

Part Perfect

The first two underlined words in each sentence name a part and a whole. The third underlined word names another part. Complete each sentence with a word that names the second whole.

> **Tip** ✓
>
> A <u>lobe</u> is to an <u>ear</u> as a <u>nostril</u> is to a <u>nose</u>.
>
> Say to yourself: A lobe is a part of an ear, and a nostril is a part of a nose.

1. A <u>statue</u> is to a <u>museum</u> as a <u>dictionary</u> is to a _____.
   - Ⓐ library
   - Ⓑ student
   - Ⓒ book

2. A <u>lung</u> is to a <u>mammal</u> as a <u>gill</u> is to a _____.
   - Ⓐ breathe
   - Ⓑ bird
   - Ⓒ fish

3. A <u>stanza</u> is to a <u>poem</u> as a <u>paragraph</u> is to a _____.
   - Ⓐ glossary
   - Ⓑ story
   - Ⓒ verse

4. A <u>paw</u> is to a <u>cat</u> as a <u>hoof</u> is to a _____.
   - Ⓐ dog
   - Ⓑ horse
   - Ⓒ claw

5. A <u>periscope</u> is to a <u>sub</u> as a <u>speedometer</u> is to a _____.
   - Ⓐ highway
   - Ⓑ car
   - Ⓒ telescope

6. A <u>second</u> is to a <u>minute</u> as a <u>pint</u> is to a _____.
   - Ⓐ hour
   - Ⓑ quart
   - Ⓒ cream

7. A <u>rudder</u> is to a <u>boat</u> as a <u>handlebar</u> is to a _____.
   - Ⓐ bike
   - Ⓑ basket
   - Ⓒ ship

8. A <u>faucet</u> is to a <u>sink</u> as a <u>nozzle</u> is to a _____.
   - Ⓐ shower
   - Ⓑ bathroom
   - Ⓒ drain

THINK!
Read your answers to a partner.
Explain why you chose them.

Part/Whole Relationships

Picks for Parts

Read the first word pair. Write a word from the box to complete the second word pair.

Tip ✓

ceiling : room :: lid : pot

Say to yourself: A ceiling is part of a room, and a lid is part of a pot.

W O R D   **B O X**

bird	brood	elevator	constellation
legislature	gas station	castle	skate

---

1. safe : bank :: pump : _____

2. snout : pig :: beak : _____

3. runner : sled :: blade : _____

4. daughter : family :: representative : _____

5. key : typewriter :: button : _____

6. puppy : litter :: chick : _____

7. steeple : church :: turret : _____

8. ship : fleet :: star : _____

THINK!
Read your answers to a partner.
Explain why you chose them.

Part/Whole Relationships

Name _____

Matching Pairs

Read each word pair. Choose the word pair that is related in the same way.

Tip ✔

brim : hat :: fringe : scarf

Say to yourself: A brim is part of a hat, and a fringe is part of a scarf.

1. desk : classroom :: _____
   - Ⓐ bookcase : library
   - Ⓑ sink : tub
   - Ⓒ bell : ring

2. segment : line :: _____
   - Ⓐ straight : curved
   - Ⓑ minus : less
   - Ⓒ angle : triangle

3. sole : shoe :: _____
   - Ⓐ sit : stand
   - Ⓑ wool : leather
   - Ⓒ thumb : glove

4. flap : envelope :: _____
   - Ⓐ lid : box
   - Ⓑ stamp : mailbox
   - Ⓒ send : receive

5. marcher : parade :: _____
   - Ⓐ drum : horn
   - Ⓑ clown : circus
   - Ⓒ band : music

6. title : story :: _____
   - Ⓐ editorial : opinion
   - Ⓑ headline : article
   - Ⓒ tale : legend

7. lamb : flock :: _____
   - Ⓐ rooster : hen
   - Ⓑ coyote : pack
   - Ⓒ two : pair

8. neck : giraffe :: _____
   - Ⓐ foot : snake
   - Ⓑ trunk : elephant
   - Ⓒ hippo : large

THINK!
Tell a partner how the word pairs you did not choose are related.

Review

Name the Relationship

Read the first word pair. Write the phrase that tells how the words are related. Then choose the correct word to complete the analogy.

Relationship :	Same Class	Part/Whole

1. swimmer : diver :: gorilla : _____   Relationship _____
   Ⓐ banana   Ⓑ orangutan   Ⓒ water

2. prong : fork :: rim : _____   Relationship _____
   Ⓐ napkin   Ⓑ edge   Ⓒ bowl

3. refrigerator : oven :: suitcase : _____   Relationship _____
   Ⓐ clothes   Ⓑ trip   Ⓒ trunk

4. plateau : mountain :: donut : _____   Relationship _____
   Ⓐ delicious   Ⓑ muffin   Ⓒ picnic

5. antlers : deer :: pouch : _____   Relationship _____
   Ⓐ kangaroo   Ⓑ mailbag   Ⓒ food

6. shell : turtle :: roof : _____   Relationship _____
   Ⓐ lion   Ⓑ house   Ⓒ crab

7. washcloth : towel :: pecan : _____   Relationship _____
   Ⓐ raisin   Ⓑ shell   Ⓒ almond

8. day : week :: decade : _____   Relationship _____
   Ⓐ weekend   Ⓑ year   Ⓒ century

THINK!
Tell a partner why it is important to know how the words in the first pair are related.

Synonyms

Similar Meanings

Words that have almost the same meanings are called synonyms. Rewrite each sentence using a synonym from the box in place of the underlined word.

W O R D				B O X
	rapidly	emerge	numerous	
	predator	species	exotic	

1. A rain forest has <u>many</u> kinds of trees and plants.

_____

2. Vegetation grows <u>quickly</u> in a rain forest.

_____

3. Many <u>unusual</u> creatures live there.

_____

4. Some <u>kinds</u> of animals are not found anywhere else.

_____

5. The clouded leopard is a <u>hunter</u> in the forests of Southeast Asia.

_____

6. The tallest trees <u>sprout</u> above the jungle like big umbrellas.

_____

THINK!
What other synonyms could you use for each word?

Synonyms

Synonym Sentences

Choose the correct word to complete each sentence.

1. <u>Glad</u> is like <u>happy</u>, and <u>enormous</u> is like _____.
   (A) huge   (B) elephant   (C) giggle

2. <u>Chatty</u> is like <u>talkative</u>, and <u>quietly</u> is like _____.
   (A) silently   (B) noisily   (C) quickly

3. <u>Polite</u> is like <u>courteous</u>, and <u>old</u> is like _____.
   (A) rude   (B) modern   (C) ancient

4. <u>Shy</u> is like <u>timid</u>, and <u>top</u> is like _____.
   (A) meek   (B) summit   (C) bottom

5. <u>Happiness</u> is like <u>joy</u>, and <u>broad</u> is like _____.
   (A) wide   (B) narrow   (C) sorrow

6. <u>Slice</u> is like <u>cut</u>, and <u>inspect</u> is like _____.
   (A) break   (B) examine   (C) ignore

7. <u>Real</u> is like <u>genuine</u>, and <u>fake</u> is like _____.
   (A) foolish   (B) true   (C) artificial

8. <u>Dreary</u> is like <u>dismal</u>, and <u>creek</u> is like _____.
   (A) bright   (B) creak   (C) brook

THINK!
Read your answers to a partner.
Explain why you did not choose the other words.

Synonyms

Similar and Alike

The first two underlined words in each sentence name synonyms. Complete each sentence with a synonym for the third underlined word.

> **Tip** ✔
>
> A <u>lad</u> is to a <u>boy</u> as a <u>baby</u> is to an <u>infant</u>.
>
> Say to yourself: A lad is the same as a boy, and a baby is the same as an infant.

1. A <u>path</u> is to a <u>trail</u> as <u>fun</u> is to _____.
   - Ⓐ amusement
   - Ⓑ work
   - Ⓒ hike

2. <u>Damp</u> is to <u>moist</u> as <u>dry</u> is to _____.
   - Ⓐ cold
   - Ⓑ arid
   - Ⓒ wet

3. <u>Feel</u> is to <u>touch</u> as <u>discover</u> is to _____.
   - Ⓐ hear
   - Ⓑ find
   - Ⓒ lose

4. A <u>basement</u> is to a <u>cellar</u> as a <u>monarch</u> is to a _____.
   - Ⓐ subject
   - Ⓑ ruler
   - Ⓒ servant

5. <u>Firm</u> is to <u>hard</u> as <u>stocky</u> is to _____.
   - Ⓐ soft
   - Ⓑ sweet
   - Ⓒ sturdy

6. <u>Fragile</u> is to <u>delicate</u> as <u>incredible</u> is to _____.
   - Ⓐ unbelievable
   - Ⓑ weak
   - Ⓒ silly

7. <u>Three</u> is to <u>trio</u> as <u>schedule</u> is to _____.
   - Ⓐ timetable
   - Ⓑ four
   - Ⓒ late

8. <u>Neglect</u> is to <u>ignore</u> as <u>buy</u> is to _____.
   - Ⓐ forget
   - Ⓑ purchase
   - Ⓒ sell

THINK!
Read your answers to a partner.
Explain why you chose them.

Synonyms

Name _____

Synonym Pick

Read each word pair. Write a word from the box to complete the second word pair.

Tip ✔

beginning : start :: look : glance

Say to yourself: A beginning is the same as a start, and a look is the same as a glance.

W O R D					B O X
	consider	pleased	tote	state	
	require	kids	assist	alter	

1. own : possess :: say : _____

2. find : locate :: think : _____

3. grow : increase :: change : _____

4. depart : leave :: carry : _____

5. try : attempt :: need : _____

6. frequently : often :: delighted : _____

7. devour : eat :: help : _____

8. work : labor :: children : _____

THINK!
Read your answers to a partner.
Explain why you chose them.

Synonyms

Pairs of Pairs

Read each word pair. Choose the word pair that is related in the same way.

> **Tip** ✓
>
> one : single :: piece : portion
> Say to yourself: One means the same as single, and piece means the same as portion.

1. grab : seize :: _____
   - Ⓐ lose : find
   - Ⓑ teeth : mouth
   - Ⓒ make : construct

2. easy : simple :: _____
   - Ⓐ tired : restless
   - Ⓑ corner : square
   - Ⓒ careful : cautious

3. wait : pause :: _____
   - Ⓐ answer : ask
   - Ⓑ stop : halt
   - Ⓒ snow : cold

4. remember : recall :: _____
   - Ⓐ collect : gather
   - Ⓑ break : fix
   - Ⓒ hub : wheel

5. rubbish : trash :: _____
   - Ⓐ chore : task
   - Ⓑ doctor : nurse
   - Ⓒ help : hinder

6. modest : humble :: _____
   - Ⓐ right : wrong
   - Ⓑ mad : furious
   - Ⓒ warm : warmer

7. cab : taxi :: _____
   - Ⓐ agreement : treaty
   - Ⓑ eel : slippery
   - Ⓒ smile : frown

8. drowsy : sleepy :: _____
   - Ⓐ famous : unknown
   - Ⓑ bed: soft
   - Ⓒ upset : worried

THINK!
Read your answers to a partner. Explain how the word pairs you did not choose are related.

Review

● ●

What's the Relationship?

Write the phrase from the box that tells how the first two words are related.
Then choose the correct word to complete the second word pair.

Relationship:	Same Class	Part/Whole	Synonyms

1. fat : plump :: weak : _____   Relationship _____
   Ⓐ strong   Ⓑ feeble   Ⓒ thick

2. television : radio :: spring : _____   Relationship _____
   Ⓐ fall   Ⓑ warm   Ⓒ hour

3. shell : nut :: cover : _____   Relationship _____
   Ⓐ jacket   Ⓑ book   Ⓒ acorn

4. hurry : rush :: ask : _____   Relationship _____
   Ⓐ speed   Ⓑ answer   Ⓒ inquire

5. wing : plane :: wheel : _____   Relationship _____
   Ⓐ fly   Ⓑ rowboat   Ⓒ truck

6. pancake : waffle :: lipstick : _____   Relationship _____
   Ⓐ red   Ⓑ rouge   Ⓒ syrup

7. wealthy : rich :: refuse : _____   Relationship _____
   Ⓐ reject   Ⓑ acquire   Ⓒ poor

8. index : book :: hinge : _____   Relationship _____
   Ⓐ read   Ⓑ hang   Ⓒ door

THINK!
Explain to a partner how you chose each answer.

Antonyms

Opposite Meanings

Words that have opposite meanings are called antonyms. Rewrite each sentence using an antonym from the box in place of the underlined word.

W O R D				B O X
	late	down	dawn	
	hot	good-bye	clean	

1. Nathan woke up at <u>dusk</u>.

_____

2. He didn't want to be <u>punctual</u> for his appointment.

_____

3. He washed his face with <u>cold</u> water.

_____

4. Quickly, he put on some <u>dirty</u> clothes.

_____

5. Then he dashed <u>up</u> to the kitchen for breakfast.

_____

6. As Nathan left the house, he called "<u>hello</u>" to his parents.

_____

THINK!
How do the words you used change
the meaning of each sentence?

29

Antonyms

Choosing Opposites

Choose the correct word to complete each sentence.

1. <u>Risky</u> is the opposite of <u>safe</u>, and <u>generous</u> is the opposite of _____.
   Ⓐ helpful   Ⓑ selfish   Ⓒ scary

2. <u>Cause</u> is the opposite of <u>prevent</u>, and <u>hurry</u> is the opposite of _____.
   Ⓐ happen   Ⓑ destroy   Ⓒ linger

3. <u>Help</u> is the opposite of <u>hinder</u>, and <u>lose</u> is the opposite of _____.
   Ⓐ recover   Ⓑ forget   Ⓒ assist

4. <u>Outside</u> is the opposite of <u>inside</u>, and <u>over</u> is the opposite of _____.
   Ⓐ under   Ⓑ again   Ⓒ into

5. <u>Whisper</u> is the opposite of <u>shout</u>, and <u>care</u> is the opposite of _____.
   Ⓐ talk   Ⓑ maintain   Ⓒ neglect

6. <u>Cheap</u> is the opposite of <u>expensive</u>, and <u>polite</u> is the opposite of _____.
   Ⓐ costly   Ⓑ rude   Ⓒ well-mannered

7. <u>Quiet</u> is the opposite of <u>noisy</u>, and <u>calm</u> is the opposite of _____.
   Ⓐ soft   Ⓑ peaceful   Ⓒ nervous

8. <u>Open</u> is the opposite of <u>shut</u>, and <u>public</u> is the opposite of _____.
   Ⓐ free   Ⓑ private   Ⓒ people

THINK!
Read your answers to a partner.
Explain why you did not choose the other words.

Antonyms

Antonym Sentences

The first two underlined words in each sentence name antonyms. Complete each sentence with an antonym for the third underlined word.

> **Tip** ✔
> Smile is to frown as powerful is to weak.
> Say to yourself: Smile is the opposite of frown,
> and powerful is the opposite of weak.

1. Valuable is to worthless as comic is to _____.
   Ⓐ funny   Ⓑ tragic   Ⓒ worthy

2. Professional is to amateur as bold is to _____.
   Ⓐ grin   Ⓑ volunteer   Ⓒ bashful

3. Low is to high as southeast is to _____.
   Ⓐ northwest   Ⓑ southern   Ⓒ north

4. Crowded is to empty as here is to _____.
   Ⓐ there   Ⓑ where   Ⓒ full

5. Forbid is to allow as win is to _____.
   Ⓐ lose   Ⓑ permit   Ⓒ won

6. Drowsy is to alert as antique is to _____.
   Ⓐ ready   Ⓑ pretty   Ⓒ modern

7. Occupied is to vacant as rough is to _____.
   Ⓐ old   Ⓑ gentle   Ⓒ new

8. Talkative is to silent as wise is to _____.
   Ⓐ smart   Ⓑ chatty   Ⓒ foolish

THINK!
Read your answers to a partner.
Explain why you chose them.

Antonyms

Antonym Search

Read each word pair. Write a word from the box to complete the second word pair.

Tip ✔
today : yesterday :: health : sickness
Say to yourself: Today is the opposite of yesterday, and health is the opposite of sickness.

W O R D

nonsense	never	bright	late
evening	carelessness	include	complete

B O X

1. hope : despair :: perfection : _____

2. formal : informal :: dreary : _____

3. group : solo :: always : _____

4. inaccurate : correct :: sense : _____

5. light : dark :: unfinished : _____

6. annoyed : pleased :: early : _____

7. drought : flood :: morning : _____

8. sloppy : neat :: exclude : _____

THINK!
Read your answers to a partner.
Explain why you chose them.

Antonym

Perfect Pairs

Read each word pair. Choose the word pair that is related in the same way.

Tip ✔

true : fanciful :: present : absent
Say to yourself: True is the opposite of fanciful,
and present is the opposite of absent.

1. majority : minority :: _____
   Ⓐ more : most   Ⓑ enter : entrance   Ⓒ increase : dwindle

2. scorn : praise :: _____
   Ⓐ whistle : sing   Ⓑ room : hotel   Ⓒ problem : solution

3. even : odd :: _____
   Ⓐ him : her   Ⓑ good : well   Ⓒ three : four

4. active : passive :: _____
   Ⓐ torment : distress   Ⓑ loose : tight   Ⓒ witty : funny

5. unwilling : agreeable :: _____
   Ⓐ disclose : hide   Ⓑ lobe : ear   Ⓒ unsafe : risky

6. eager : reluctant :: _____
   Ⓐ together : apart   Ⓑ excellent : good   Ⓒ bark : tree

7. leader : follower :: _____
   Ⓐ seed : plant   Ⓑ first : last   Ⓒ renew : restore

8. kind : cruel:: _____
   Ⓐ bad : worse   Ⓑ something : nothing   Ⓒ leopard : lion

THINK!
Read your answers to a partner.
Explain how the word pairs you did not
choose are related.

Review

Reviewing Relationships

Write the phrase from the box that tells how the first two words are related. Then choose the correct word to complete the analogy.

Relationship:	Same Class	Part/Whole
	Synonyms	Antonyms

1. log : woodpile :: poem : _____   Relationship _____
   Ⓐ rhyme   Ⓑ anthology   Ⓒ tree

2. commercial : ad :: legend : _____   Relationship _____
   Ⓐ tale   Ⓑ television   Ⓒ storyteller

3. ordinary : unique :: graceful : _____   Relationship _____
   Ⓐ clumsy   Ⓑ dancer   Ⓒ unusual

4. lily : rose :: carnival : _____   Relationship _____
   Ⓐ excitement   Ⓑ daisy   Ⓒ circus

5. test : experiment :: entertain : _____   Relationship _____
   Ⓐ fail   Ⓑ amuse   Ⓒ bore

6. laughter : tears :: terrify : _____   Relationship _____
   Ⓐ frighten   Ⓑ comfort   Ⓒ giggle

7. glass : mirror :: mast : _____   Relationship _____
   Ⓐ sailboat   Ⓑ window   Ⓒ pole

8. complicated : simple :: feast : _____   Relationship _____
   Ⓐ meal   Ⓑ difficult   Ⓒ famine

THINK!
Explain to a partner how you chose each answer.

Homophones

Name _____

They're There

Words that sound alike but have different spellings and meanings are called homophones. *Their*, *there*, and *they're* are homophones. Write a homophone for each word below. Use the words in the box.

W O R D				B O X
two	whole	know	won	
mane	grown	plain	steal	
flower	seen	ant	dear	
road	hear	through	see	

1. main _____

2. groan _____

3. scene _____

4. to _____

5. hole _____

6. no _____

7. plane _____

8. flour _____

9. rode _____

10. one _____

11. steel _____

12. here _____

13. sea _____

14. aunt _____

15. threw _____

16. deer _____

THINK!
What other homophones do you know? _____

Homophones

Homophone Sentences
Choose the correct word to complete each sentence.

1. <u>Real</u> sounds like <u>reel</u>, and <u>stare</u> sounds like _____.
   - Ⓐ step
   - Ⓑ star
   - Ⓒ stair

2. <u>Beach</u> sounds like <u>beech</u>, and <u>foul</u> sounds like _____.
   - Ⓐ fowl
   - Ⓑ foal
   - Ⓒ bird

3. <u>Stake</u> sounds like <u>steak</u>, and <u>profit</u> sounds like _____.
   - Ⓐ product
   - Ⓑ prophet
   - Ⓒ money

4. <u>Insight</u> sounds like <u>incite</u>, and <u>coarse</u> sounds like _____.
   - Ⓐ court
   - Ⓑ rough
   - Ⓒ course

5. <u>By</u> sounds like <u>buy</u>, and <u>build</u> sounds like _____.
   - Ⓐ bull
   - Ⓑ billed
   - Ⓒ purchase

6. <u>Hair</u> sounds like <u>hare</u>, and <u>herd</u> sounds like _____.
   - Ⓐ heard
   - Ⓑ hear
   - Ⓒ animal

7. <u>Week</u> sounds like <u>weak</u>, and <u>past</u> sounds like _____.
   - Ⓐ path
   - Ⓑ before
   - Ⓒ passed

8. <u>Toe</u> sounds like <u>tow</u>, and <u>waste</u> sounds like _____.
   - Ⓐ wash
   - Ⓑ waist
   - Ⓒ trash

THINK!
Write a sentence using each word you wrote.
Then write a sentence using its homophone.

Homophones

Sound-Alike Words

The first two underlined words in each sentence name homophones. Complete each sentence with a homophone for the third underlined word.

> **Tip ✓**
>
> <u>Meat</u> is to <u>meet</u> as <u>sail</u> is to <u>sale</u>.
>
> Say to yourself: Meat and meet sound the same, so sail and sale must sound the same.

1. <u>New</u> is to <u>knew</u> as <u>side</u> is to _____.
   - Ⓐ know
   - Ⓑ sign
   - Ⓒ sighed

2. <u>Tale</u> is to <u>tail</u> as <u>so</u> is to _____.
   - Ⓐ sew
   - Ⓑ some
   - Ⓒ story

3. <u>Four</u> is to <u>for</u> as <u>sell</u> is to _____.
   - Ⓐ cell
   - Ⓑ buy
   - Ⓒ fore

4. <u>Brake</u> is to <u>break</u> as <u>not</u> is to _____.
   - Ⓐ fix
   - Ⓑ no
   - Ⓒ knot

5. <u>Some</u> is to <u>sum</u> as <u>sealing</u> is to _____.
   - Ⓐ seating
   - Ⓑ ceiling
   - Ⓒ floor

6. <u>Dye</u> is to <u>die</u> as <u>board</u> is to _____.
   - Ⓐ born
   - Ⓑ dull
   - Ⓒ bored

7. <u>Cent</u> is to <u>scent</u> as <u>creek</u> is to _____.
   - Ⓐ creak
   - Ⓑ sent
   - Ⓒ brook

8. <u>Heel</u> is to <u>he'll</u> as <u>our</u> is to _____.
   - Ⓐ out
   - Ⓑ hour
   - Ⓒ heal

THINK!
Write a sentence using each word you wrote.
Then write a sentence using its homophone.

Homophones

○ ○

Homophone Picks

Read each word pair. Write a word from the box to complete the second word pair.

Tip ✓

pail : pale :: pear : pair

Say to yourself: Pail sounds the same as pale,

so pear must sound the same as pair.

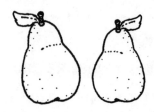

W O R D	wade	lessen	wring	pierce	hoarse	B O X
	peace	listen	would	pause	raise	

---

1. role : roll :: lesson : _____

2. sight : site :: horse : _____

3. plain : plane :: weighed : _____

4. night : knight :: ring : _____

5. peek : peak :: wood : _____

6. straight : strait :: piece : _____

7. right : write :: rays : _____

8. rain : reign :: paws : _____

THINK!

Write a sentence using each word you wrote.
Then write a sentence using its homophone.

Homophones

Homophone Pairs

Read each word pair. Choose the word pair that is related in the same way.

> **Tip** ✔
> in : inn :: pain : pane
> Say to yourself: In sounds the same as inn so pain must sound the same as pane.

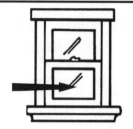

1. cheep : cheap :: _____
   - Ⓐ ride : rid
   - Ⓑ case : chase
   - Ⓒ band : banned

2. bury : berry :: _____
   - Ⓐ close : clothes
   - Ⓑ cherry : cheer
   - Ⓒ rat : rate

3. ate : eight :: _____
   - Ⓐ eat : food
   - Ⓑ nine : ten
   - Ⓒ bold : bowled

4. bee : be :: _____
   - Ⓐ chews : choose
   - Ⓑ busy : buzz
   - Ⓒ lip : mouth

5. cellar : seller :: _____
   - Ⓐ buyer : buy
   - Ⓑ loot : look
   - Ⓒ principle : principal

6. fir : fur :: _____
   - Ⓐ tree : three
   - Ⓑ snooze : nap
   - Ⓒ dew : due

7. made : maid :: _____
   - Ⓐ poke : punch
   - Ⓑ rap : wrap
   - Ⓒ build : built

8. pour : pore :: _____
   - Ⓐ loan : lone
   - Ⓑ ball : bail
   - Ⓒ chop : cut

THINK!
Explain to a partner how you chose each answer.

Review

Name _____

Identifying Relationships

Write the phrase from the box that tells how the first two words are related. Then write the correct word to complete the analogy.

Relationship:	Same Class	Part/Whole	Synonyms
	Antonyms	Homophones	

1. weight : wait :: gilt : _____   Relationship _____
   Ⓐ wave   Ⓑ guilt   Ⓒ gill

2. work : play :: deep : _____   Relationship _____
   Ⓐ shallow   Ⓑ dive   Ⓒ job

3. elm : pine :: bee : _____   Relationship _____
   Ⓐ birch   Ⓑ honey   Ⓒ beetle

4. seam : seem :: I : _____   Relationship _____
   Ⓐ me   Ⓑ eye   Ⓒ you

5. kernel : corn :: seed : _____   Relationship _____
   Ⓐ soil   Ⓑ water   Ⓒ watermelon

6. forest : woods :: field : _____   Relationship _____
   Ⓐ meadow   Ⓑ flower   Ⓒ farmer

7. leave : arrive :: asked : _____   Relationship _____
   Ⓐ go   Ⓑ told   Ⓒ inquired

8. wheel : we'll :: hall : _____   Relationship _____
   Ⓐ help   Ⓑ hill   Ⓒ haul

THINK!
Explain to a partner how you chose each answer.

40

Class and Example

Class Names

Things can be grouped or classed together because they are alike in some way.
Write two examples from the box for each class below.

W O R D					B O X
	oak	screwdriver	swimming	purple	
	hill	brown	soccer	grape	
	wrench	violinist	drummer	valley	
	watermelon	poppy	spruce	iris	

1. Colors _____   _____

2. Trees _____   _____

3. Sports _____   _____

4. Musicians _____   _____

5. Flowers _____   _____

6. Tools _____   _____

7. Fruits _____   _____

8. Landforms _____   _____

THINK!
Think of another example for each class.

Class and Example

In the Class

Choose the correct word to complete each sentence.

1. A <u>desk</u> is an example of <u>furniture</u>, and a <u>doll</u> is an example of a _____.
   Ⓐ table   Ⓑ toy   Ⓒ girl

2. A <u>fork</u> is an example of a <u>utensil</u>, and a <u>hammer</u> is an example of a _____.
   Ⓐ tool   Ⓑ saw   Ⓒ spoon

3. A <u>spaniel</u> is an example of a <u>dog</u>, and a <u>goose</u> is an example of a _____.
   Ⓐ fowl   Ⓑ duck   Ⓒ puppy

4. <u>Juice</u> is an example of a <u>liquid</u>, and <u>mountain</u> is an example of a _____.
   Ⓐ drink   Ⓑ tall   Ⓒ landform

5. <u>Pie</u> is an example of a <u>dessert</u>, and <u>cheddar</u> is an example of a _____.
   Ⓐ cake   Ⓑ bread   Ⓒ cheese

6. <u>Spain</u> is an example of a <u>country</u>, and <u>Africa</u> is an example of a _____.
   Ⓐ Europe   Ⓑ town   Ⓒ continent

7. A <u>mare</u> is an example of a <u>female</u>, and a <u>carrot</u> is an example of a _____.
   Ⓐ vegetable   Ⓑ horse   Ⓒ male

8. A <u>hat</u> is an example of <u>clothing</u>, and a <u>bracelet</u> is an example of _____.
   Ⓐ pins   Ⓑ jewelry   Ⓒ glasses

THINK!
Read your answers to a partner.
Explain why you did not choose the other words.

Class and Example

Name _____

What's the Class?

The first two underlined words name an example and the class it belongs to.
Complete each sentence with the class for the third underlined word.

> **Tip** ✔
> Baseball is to sports as dragonfly is to insect.
> Say to yourself: Baseball is an example of a sport,
> and a dragonfly is an example of an insect.

1. Five is to number as a bus is to _____.
   Ⓐ riders   Ⓑ vehicle   Ⓒ cars

2. A steak is to meat as a banana is to _____.
   Ⓐ fruit   Ⓑ monkey   Ⓒ yellow

3. A plumber is to worker as an almond is to _____.
   Ⓐ nut   Ⓑ candy   Ⓒ cashews

4. An owl is to bird as a snake is to _____.
   Ⓐ long   Ⓑ python   Ⓒ reptile

5. A novel is to literature as a dime is to _____.
   Ⓐ ten   Ⓑ coin   Ⓒ nickel

6. A comma is to punctuation as a yacht is to _____.
   Ⓐ water   Ⓑ capital   Ⓒ boat

7. A foal is to newborn as a toaster is to _____.
   Ⓐ horse   Ⓑ appliance   Ⓒ breakfast

8. A train is to transportation as a telephone is to _____.
   Ⓐ friend   Ⓑ travel   Ⓒ communication

THINK!
Read your answers to a partner.
Explain why you chose them.

Class and Example

Match the Class

Read each word pair. Write a word from the box to complete the second word pair.

> **Tip** ✓
>
> happy : feeling :: linen : fabric
> Say to yourself: Happy is an example of a feeling,
> and linen is an example of a fabric.

W O R D	container	insect	musician	family	**B O X**
	rock	river	storm	fuel	

1. trumpet : horn :: father : _____

2. linguine : pasta :: cyclone : _____

3. tuna : fish :: quartz : _____

4. dandelion : weed :: box : _____

5. frog : amphibian : centipede : _____

6. measles : disease :: coal : _____

7. Seattle : city :: Hudson : _____

8. nimbus : cloud :: pianist : _____

 THINK!
Read your answers to a partner.
Explain why you chose them.

Class and Example

Pairing Up
Read each word pair. Choose the word pair that is related in the same way.

> **Tip** ✓
>
> steel : metal :: tent : shelter
> Say to yourself: Steel is an example of metal,
> and a tent is an example of a shelter.

1. carnation : flower :: _____
   - Ⓐ inch : measurement
   - Ⓑ leg : arm
   - Ⓒ seed : root

2. tea : drink :: _____
   - Ⓐ canteen : water
   - Ⓑ dancer : performer
   - Ⓒ warm : cool

3. Tuesday : day :: _____
   - Ⓐ Tucson : Phoenix
   - Ⓑ year : decade
   - Ⓒ April : month

4. east : direction :: _____
   - Ⓐ lost : found
   - Ⓑ emerald : gem
   - Ⓒ pencil : write

5. Pluto : planet :: _____
   - Ⓐ pediatrician : doctor
   - Ⓑ Mars : Saturn
   - Ⓒ spaceship : astronaut

6. Betty : name :: _____
   - Ⓐ pins : needles
   - Ⓑ spring : season
   - Ⓒ girl : boy

7. hopscotch : game :: _____
   - Ⓐ ball : bat
   - Ⓑ jump : leap
   - Ⓒ rooster : male

8. Everest : mountain :: _____
   - Ⓐ wheat : grain
   - Ⓑ tacks : tax
   - Ⓒ sea : ocean

THINK!
Read your answers to a partner. Explain how
the word pairs you did not choose are related.

Review

Recognizing Relationships Part I

Write the phrase from the box that tells how the first two words are related.
Then choose the correct word to complete the analogy.

Relationships:	Same Class	Synonyms	Homophones
	Part/Whole	Antonyms	Class and Example

1. bulldozer : machine :: symphony : _____   Relationship _____
   Ⓐ music   Ⓑ sympathy   Ⓒ crane

2. peaceful : calm :: disturbed : _____   Relationship _____
   Ⓐ warning   Ⓑ upset   Ⓒ relaxed

3. red : green :: niece : _____   Relationship _____
   Ⓐ relative   Ⓑ yellow   Ⓒ nephew

4. hero : villain :: friend : _____   Relationship _____
   Ⓐ heroine   Ⓑ pal   Ⓒ foe

5. ore : or :: higher : _____   Relationship _____
   Ⓐ lower   Ⓑ hire   Ⓒ hi

6. detective : sleuth :: shack : _____   Relationship _____
   Ⓐ spy   Ⓑ mansion   Ⓒ hut

7. bead : necklace :: dial : _____   Relationship _____
   Ⓐ watch   Ⓑ neck   Ⓒ earring

8. giant : dwarf :: liquid : _____   Relationship _____
   Ⓐ wet   Ⓑ solid   Ⓒ water

THINK!
Explain to a partner how you chose each answer.

Class and Example

Name _____

Write the phrase from the box that tells how the first two words are related.
Then write the correct word to complete the analogy.

Relationships:	Same Class	Synonyms	Homophones
	Part/Whole	Antonyms	Class and Example

1. duck : goose :: plate : _____   Relationship _____

   Ⓐ bowl   Ⓑ place   Ⓒ bird

2. shingle : roof :: brick : _____   Relationship _____

   Ⓐ window   Ⓑ red   Ⓒ house

3. weave : we've :: rose : _____   Relationship _____

   Ⓐ fell   Ⓑ rows   Ⓒ rode

4. hungry : full :: surplus : _____   Relationship _____

   Ⓐ shortage   Ⓑ extra   Ⓒ meal

5. camel : horse :: slide : _____   Relationship _____

   Ⓐ side   Ⓑ seesaw   Ⓒ slip

6. ruler : tool :: lettuce : _____   Relationship _____

   Ⓐ leaf   Ⓑ fruit   Ⓒ vegetable

7. thief : robber :: child : _____   Relationship _____

   Ⓐ adult   Ⓑ youngster   Ⓒ family

8. spine : cactus :: quill : _____   Relationship _____

   Ⓐ porcupine   Ⓑ quilt   Ⓒ fur

THINK!
Explain to a partner how you chose each answer.

Answers

page 8 1. Dogs 2. Weather 3. Drinks 4. Parts of the Face 5. Meats 6. Liquid Measurements 7. Landforms 8. Geometric Figures

page 9 1. inform (topple) 2. stamen (macaw) 3. pond (inform) 4. temple (stamen) 5. macaw (temple) 6. topple (pond)

page 10 Answers may vary. Possible: 1. They both sail in the air. 2. They both keep time. 3. You can read them both for the news. 4. They are both musical instruments with keys. 5. They are both enclosed bodies of water. 6. Cars can drive on both. 7. You can sleep on them. 8. You wear them on your head.

page 11 1. imaginary/make-believe 2. solid/liquid 3. allow/permit 4. terrier/retriever 5. here/hear 6. snake/reptile 7. stroll/walk 8. cord/lamp

page 12 1. E, 2. I, 3. F, 4. H, 5. A, 6. B, 7. J, 8. D, 9. G, 10. C

page 13 1. C, 2. A, 3. A, 4. C, 5. B, 6. C, 7. B, 8. A

page 14 1. C, 2. B, 3. A, 4. A, 5. C, 6. B, 7. B, 8. A

page 15 1. apple 2. hoe 3. goat 4. train 5. peninsula 6. mumps 7. lobster 8. period

page 16 1. C, 2. C, 3. B, 4. A, 5. C, 6. B, 7. C, 8. C

page 17 1. – 5. Students should note that in each analogy, the first item in the word pair is a part of the second item.

page 18 1. B, 2. A, 3. C, 4. A, 5. C, 6. A, 7. B, 8. B

page 19 1. A, 2. C, 3. B, 4. B, 5. B, 6. B, 7. A, 8. A

page 20 1. gas station 2. bird 3. skate 4. legislature 5. elevator 6. brood 7. castle 8. constellation

page 21 1. A, 2. C, 3. C, 4. A, 5. B, 6. B, 7. B, 8. B

page 22 1. B same class 2. C part/whole 3. C same class 4. B same class 5. A part/whole 6. B part/whole 7. C same class 8. C part/whole

page 23 1. numerous 2. rapidly 3. exotic 4. species 5. predator 6. emerge

page 24 1. A, 2. A, 3. C, 4. B, 5. A, 6. B, 7. C, 8. C

page 25 1. A, 2. B, 3. B, 4. B, 5. C, 6. A, 7. A, 8. B

page 26 1. state 2. consider 3. alter 4. tote 5. require 6. pleased 7. assist 8. kids

page 27 1. C, 2. C, 3. B, 4. A, 5. A, 6. B, 7. A, 8. C

page 28 1. B synonyms 2. A same class 3. B part/whole 4. C synonyms 5. C part/whole 6. B same class 7. A synonyms 8. C part/whole

page 29 1. dawn 2. late 3. hot 4. clean 5. down 6. good-bye

page 30 1. B, 2. C, 3. A, 4. A, 5. C, 6. B, 7. C, 8. B

page 31 1. B, 2. C, 3. A, 4. A, 5. A, 6. C, 7. B, 8. C

page 32 1. carelessness 2. bright 3. never 4. nonsense 5. complete 6. late 7. evening 8. include

page 33 1. C, 2. C, 3. A, 4. B, 5. A, 6. A, 7. B, 8. B

page 34 1. B part/whole 2. A synonyms 3. A antonyms 4. C same class 5. B synonyms 6. B antonyms 7. A part/whole 8. C antonyms

page 35 1. mane 2. grown 3. seen 4. two 5. whole 6. know 7. plain 8. flower 9. road 10. won 11. steal 12. hear 13. see 14. ant 15. through 16. dear

page 36 1. C, 2. A, 3. B, 4. C, 5. B, 6. A, 7. C, 8. B

page 37 1. C, 2. A, 3. A, 4. C, 5. B, 6. C, 7. A, 8. B

page 38 1. lessen 2. hoarse 3. wade 4. wring 5. would 6. peace 7. raise 8. pause

page 39 1. C, 2. A, 3. C, 4. A, 5. C, 6. C, 7. B, 8. A

page 40 1. B homophones 2. A antonyms 3. C same class 4. B homophones 5. C part/whole 6. A synonyms 7. B antonyms 8. C homophones

page 41 1. brown, purple 2. oak, spruce 3. swimming, soccer 4. violinist, drummer 5. poppy, iris 6. wrench, screwdriver 7. grape, watermelon 8. hill, valley

page 42 1. B, 2. A, 3. A, 4. C, 5. C, 6. C, 7. A, 8. B

page 43 1. B, 2. A, 3. A, 4. C, 5. B, 6. C, 7. B, 8. C

page 44 1. family 2. storm 3. rock 4. container 5. insect 6. fuel 7. river 8. musician

page 45 1. A, 2. B, 3. C, 4. B, 5. A, 6. B, 7. C, 8. A

page 46 1. A class and example 2. B synonyms 3. C same class 4. C antonyms 5. B homophones 6. C synonyms 7. A part/whole 8. B antonyms

page 47 1. A same class 2. C part/whole 3. B homophones 4. A antonyms 5. B same class 6. C class and example 7. B synonyms 8. A part/whole